·INTRODUCTION·

Even if you live in a town or a city, you may see wild animals – animals which live their own lives in parks and gardens, and even in our houses.

Most people know a mouse when they see one. (But they don't know a house mouse from a wood mouse.) Squirrels live in parks and raid bird tables in gardens. Even foxes and badgers have moved into towns. If you live in the country, or on the edge of a town, you may have a hedgehog in your garden. All these are wild animals.

It is much more interesting to watch them if you know which animals they are, and what they are doing. The book tells you about some of them, and about how they live.

The animals in this book all belong to a special group of animals called **mammals**. Mammals are animals which suckle their young: that means the young ones suck milk from their mother's nipples.

·MICE·

HOUSE MOUSE

House mice can live out of doors, but many like to live in houses. In a house, they are warm and dry in winter. And they can find food in a house – bread, cheese, cake, biscuits – and any scraps people leave lying around. They will even eat soap.

House mice leave their droppings on food. This spreads germs, so people try to get rid of the mice. But it isn't easy. They have so many babies.

Young mouse

The female – the mother mouse – makes a soft nest by tearing up pieces of paper or cloth. She has between four and eight babies, or even more.

This mouse has made her nest in a cushion. The babies are born with their eyes shut, like kittens. But they grow so fast that, when they are three weeks old, they are ready to leave the nest.

A mouse may have between four and eight families in one year. Young mice are ready to start their own families when they are six weeks old.

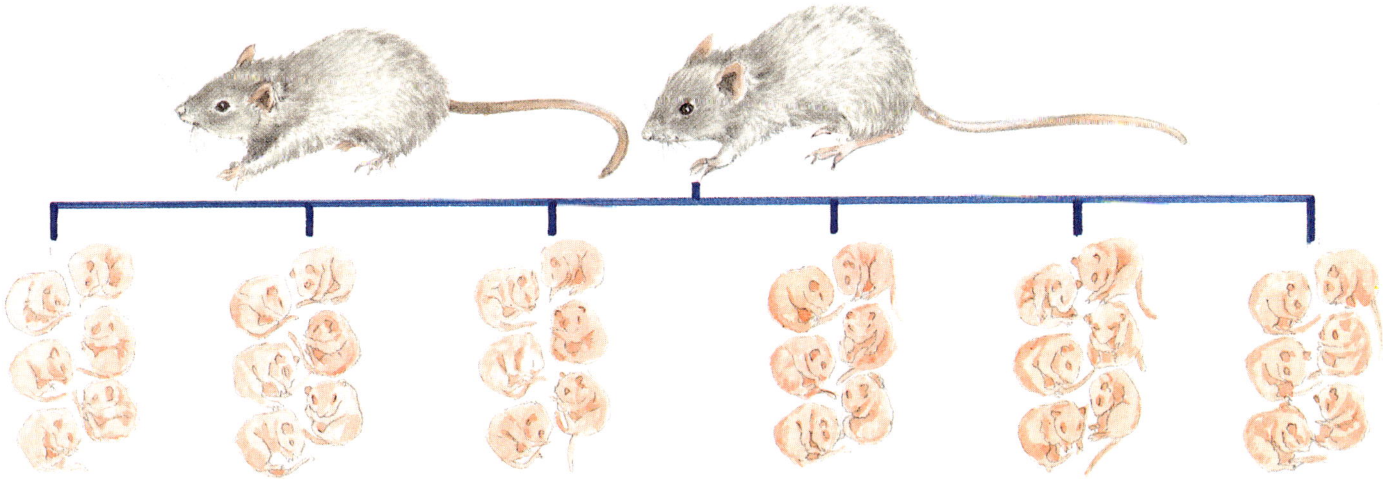

WOOD MOUSE

Wood mice live all over the countryside, in woods, fields and open spaces. They live in gardens, too, and may come into a shed, or even a house, in winter. But you don't often see them, because they only go out in the evening and at night.

Wood mice dig **burrows** underground. The mother makes a soft nest of dry grass for her babies.

The mice store food in the burrow, too. Many animals eat wood mice, so the mice hide in their burrows by day. At night, owls hunt for wood mice.

· FOXES ·

♀ Vixen

♂ Dog fox

Cubs

The male fox is called a **dog fox**.
The female is called a **vixen**.

Before the **cubs** are born, the vixen digs two or three dens (called **earths**). She chooses one for her cubs.

Inside a fox's earth

If she thinks someone has seen them, the mother fox will move the cubs to another earth, to keep them safe.

Sometimes young vixens, who were cubs last year, stay with the family. They bring food to the cubs and play with them. They look after the cubs when mother fox goes hunting for food.

Foxes eat worms, so you may see them in a field, or in a garden, in the late evening or the very early morning. Foxes are **nocturnal**. That means they are out at night and sleep for at least part of the day.

They catch mice, too, and other little animals. They can pounce, like a cat.

Each fox family has its own patch of wood and countryside, or gardens in a town, where it lives and finds its food. This is called the foxes' **territory**.

Foxes will chase strange foxes out of their territory.

Some foxes live in the countryside, and come into the town at night, looking for food. They will eat scraps from dustbins.

Foxes don't hurt cats. (If they do have a fight with a cat, the cat often wins.) But they will eat pet rabbits or guinea pigs, if they can get them. Small animals need somewhere safe to sleep at night.

When they live in a town, foxes try to find hidden places to live. They like to keep hidden as they move about, too, but they often have to move in the open.

Gardens and parks are good places for foxes. The banks along a railway line, or along a canal, are good roads for a fox.

Foxes can live until they are twelve years old, but not many live as long as that. Some are killed by cars. In the country, foxes may be hunted or shot, because farmers are afraid they may kill young lambs or chickens. Foxes may also kill and eat pheasants, which the farmers will shoot in autumn, for people to eat.

Rabbits live together in a group of burrows, called a **warren**. They come out in the morning and evening to eat the grass.

The mother rabbit makes a special burrow, where she makes a nest for her babies. She makes a lining for it with fur from her chest.

The babies feed from their mother, until they are three or four weeks old.

After three weeks, the young rabbits leave the nest in the daytime.

Outside, some rabbits are always on the look out for enemies. If a rabbit sees an enemy, he thumps the ground with his back feet. His white tail bobs up and down as he runs. These signs warn the other rabbits.

·HARES·

Hares live in fields, in the open countryside. They look very like rabbits, but they have longer legs and ears, and they don't dig burrows.

They make a kind of nest, by flattening the middle of a patch of grass. This is called a **form**. They often lie in their forms for part of the day, and are out and about in the early morning and evening. They eat grass and other plants.

A baby hare is called a **leveret**. It is born in a form in a patch of grass. Its eyes are open as soon as it is born, and it is covered in fur. The fur keeps it warm, because it has to live in an open field from the time it is born.

There are between two and four leverets. Soon after they are born, they move into small forms of their own. Hares can live three or four years, but many animals would eat a baby hare. So it keeps very still, hiding in its form.

Hares which live in the mountains grow a white coat in winter, so they can hide in the snow. All hares can run very fast, to escape from their enemies.

Mountain hare

·HEDGEHOGS·

Hedgehogs hunt at night. They eat worms, slugs, snails, beetles and other insects. Hedgehogs can live for eight years.

When a hedgehog is in danger, it curls up. Its spines will keep a dog away, but not a car. Many hedgehogs are killed by cars.

The mother hedgehog makes a nest of grass and leaves. Baby hedgehogs are born in June and July. Soon after they are born, their spines begin to push upwards through their skin.

In the autumn, a hedgehog **hibernates**. That is, it finds a sheltered place, curls up into a ball and goes into a kind of deep sleep until spring.

· MOLES ·

Moles spend most of their time underground.

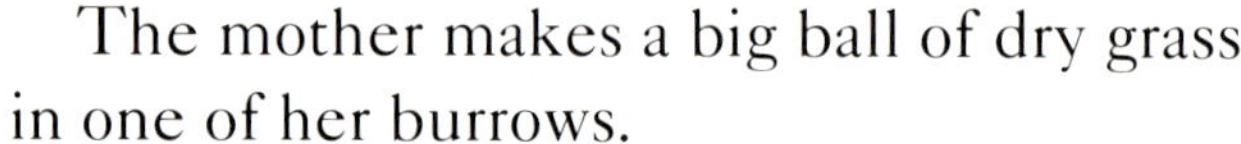

The mother makes a big ball of dry grass in one of her burrows.

A mole at work

As the mole digs its burrow, it pushes the earth up from time to time. The heaps of earth are called molehills.

A mole goes along its burrows every day, looking for worms and grubs to eat.

·BADGERS·

Badgers live in woods and fields. They are nocturnal: they only come out at night, and sleep during the daytime.

Badgers eat earthworms and insects and fruit. They will sometimes eat young rabbits, or a wild bees' nest or a wasps' nest. They love honey and eat the grubs. Their fur is so thick and strong it can protect them from stings.

Badgers live in a burrow, called a **sett**. They dig out their setts with their strong front paws. They pull dry grass and leaves inside, to make a bed. They are very clean and tidy, and often change their bedding.

A male badger is called a **boar**. A female is called a **sow**. The boar will defend his home territory against strange badgers.

Young badgers are born in spring. Some badgers live for up to fifteen years.

·SQUIRRELS·

Grey squirrel

Red squirrel

You don't often see red squirrels. Red squirrels usually live in woods. They eat the seeds of trees. (They like pine tree seeds, which they find in pine cones.)

Grey squirrels often live in parks and gardens. They eat nuts, seeds, acorns, mushrooms and buds of trees and plants. They will eat biscuits, too, and they often come to bird tables.

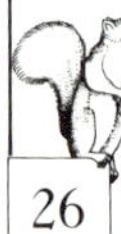

Squirrels make nests in trees, out of twigs and dry leaves. The nest is like a ball, with a big hole inside. It is called a **drey**.

Squirrels sometimes find a hole in a tree to live in. Young squirrels are born there, or in a drey, in spring. They leave the nest when their teeth are fully grown – when they are about ten weeks old.

·VOLES·

Bank voles look rather like wood mice, with rounder heads. They live among brambles, in banks, or in hedges and gardens.

Bank voles dig a burrow in the earth, and store their food there. The babies are born in the burrow.

FIELD VOLES

Field voles live in the fields. Their heads are rounder than bank voles', and they have shorter tails.

Voles have many enemies. Foxes, owls, and many other animals eat them. They can live to be about eighteen months old, but not many do.

Water voles live by rivers and ponds. Some people call them 'water rats', but they are really voles. They live on plants that grow in clean water. They are twice as big as field voles and bank voles.

Water voles make their burrows in the bank. One burrow comes out above ground, but one comes out under water. Then, if they see an enemy, they can dive into the water, and find their way safely home without being seen.